Growth Rings

Also by Christine Evans

Looking Inland
Falling Back
Cometary Phases
Island of Dark Horses
Selected Poems

Christine Evans
Growth Rings

seren

Seren is the book imprint of
Poetry Wales Press Ltd
57 Nolton Street, Bridgend, Wales, CF31 3AE
www.seren-books.com

ISBN 1-85411-402-6
A CIP record for this title is available from the British Library

The publisher acknowledges the financial assistance
of the Welsh Books Council

Printed in Hoefler by Bell and Bain, Glasgow

Cover photograph: *Arctoparmelia centrifuga* by Stephen Sharnoff

Contents

Growth Rings	7
How to Make a Pen	8
Looking Out	9
Recollection	11
A Forging	12
For Christmas	14
Inbetween	15
Rebuilding	16
Watching Skylarks	18
Bluebells in Nanhoron	19
Silver Wedding	20
Thesaurian	21
Postcard	22
In Their Chains	24
The Scent of Geraniums	25
4th June, Beijing	26
At Los Alamos	27
Shelley Solving the Great Riddle	30
Survivor	32
Plath	34
Phantoms over Wales	35
Adjusting the Focus	36
On the Train from Chester	38
Talking in the Dark	39
Mrs Crusoe	40
Harvest	41
Before the Bell	43
Giving Up	44
Not Much Like R.S. Thomas	46
Rounding	48
Safeways	49
Crossing from the Island	50
Ghost-dance of the Island Goose	51
Controlling	52
Going Over	53

Lightning	55
Out of Season	57
Before Full Reason Wakes	60
The Mariner's Last Message	61
Estuary	63
Swimmers	64
Exodus	69
The Whirlpool Arm	70
Acknowledgements	72

GROWTH RINGS

The image sent by satellite of an earthquake on the San Andreas fault.

The ground slips sideways again.
Five thousand miles away
a scientist just back from lunch
leans amazed to the radar image
growing on the screen:

whorls on a thumbtip
heart of an unfolding rose
clusters of muscle, spasming
where the hurt is most. Print-out
of a scream gathering
in the throats of houses
sliding into dust and silence.

Each earthquake dreams
creation, splitting open
to the roar of a gigantic oven.
Here, rock is reminded
how, before the mesa cities, before lights
and freeways strung the desert,
it swirled like water in a plughole;

silk for the shirring, stirred
cakemix cooking. Giant hooks
catch at our roots, question marks
folded into infinity, each tremor
insisting that we not forget
life is this, just this – cells
rippling, growing, dividing;
splitting at the fault line.

HOW TO MAKE A PEN

First, find a wing-feather
still firm and curved by the wind.
If possible still white and warm
at the tip. Goose is good; swan is better.

Harden it in water jellied with ice.
Heat sand and trickle in to fill
the hollow core, to scour it clean.
Take rock from the heart of a volcano

and with its soft grey ashes in a cloth
smooth off last stubborn strands of flesh.
Now, sharpen steel and with it make
one long slanting cut across the tip –

fine or thick according to the angle –
for the words to find their way
down the grooves blood has worn
on those journeys arcing across our sky.

Then, try your mark. Let the letters fly.

LOOKING OUT

The shortest day, and darkness gathering
already in the hollows of each wave.
A bitter easterly brings smoke and steel
and promises of ice at nightfall
to bay exhilaration
from this shore, but two old men still lean
across the sea-wall, intent as if
on salvage. As long as there is light
you will see them, silhouettes
braving the cold, looking out to sea.

And in summer, watch the faces
come alive as they run down to it
failing to see the flowers
underfoot, the peregrine that hunches
heavy with purpose on the cliff-face.
Only the smaller children
have time for the colour of the pebbles
and the detail in quiet pools
the tide abandoned. The rest of us

gorge our senses on its absolutes,
the distances that make us
less accountable. And it tastes
like something we should recognise –
not tears, not blood – an ancient
mindlessness we were once
part of. It rides the ecstasy
of smashing and never afterwards
has wounds to throb. The here and now
breaks, rolls free, in each translucent wave.

So never up, or inward; always out
as if all threat, all exploration
came from beyond. The ocean
and the stars – those outer spaces –
draw our gaze to practise losing
selves we've had so little time
to find. For this last hour, the waves
are stained with sunset, warmth they will
shake off, glittering and indifferent
as knives. The silhouettes hang on.

RECOLLECTION

Carrying coal in sacks up from the road
over snow-lit fields, my father tried to talk to me
of love and time and how in Brussels once
he strolled an avenue of lime trees late
with a Jewish girl called Rosa, on their way
to change the world
with Esperanto. That night was warm, he said,
and smelt of flowers from the opulent
dark gardens; stars and streetlights shone
so brightly through the bloom that hand in hand
they stood together islanded in lustre
and gazed up through it at the endless sky.

But from the moor
an irritable wind breathed ice
on the wet grit in my hair, my hands
ungloved, gone numb. I felt no thrill, no tragedy
to cut through the embarrassment
of hearing even passion's echo
wrung from that stooped man. I swung my hump away;
plunged on alone towards the lighted square
my mother's sourfish mouth, the bickering brood.

For twenty winters, his ashes have been scattering.

This afternoon I walk
thigh-deep in seeding grasses
just as far from the words
I thought blown away
as he from the blossom
opening to skies
without a thought of winter.

The moment turns me
in its case of ice: at its heart
white petals and his harsh-drawn breath
still labouring up the hill behind me.

A FORGING

"We think back through our mothers, if we are women."
– Virginia Woolf

Once more, it was November, and she was
stranded at the limits of our range
squirming and mewling
like the two-month too-early baby she had been
lacking the strength even
to cry. And I, as if I were her mother,
hung over the narrow bed
as if I'd played a part
in bringing her to this.

Touch may be the first and last
of solaces. I shall not easily forget
her frailty against my breast
and how it soothed her.
Her body felt all bone and air
wrapped carelessly, like a starved bird.

I had fought her power all my life.

Holding her while the injection worked
was more natural than anything we'd done
as mother and daughter. By then
I had a child myself so I knew this
was more than transferred tenderness;
something older than love.
Comfort flowed through me and I took on
all that was left of her broken hope.

Midwife, not mother, I was easing her out.

After a while, she was quiet
heavier on my arm, so I settled her
for sleep. She lay curled on her side
hands and eyes shut tight,
nuzzling oblivion. Rain was soothing
the roar of all the traffic going home
to surf on a distant reef.

I turned the light off; left her to it.

And have carried her within me
ever since, spooled small in the dark
like a sigh that cannot break.
I shall not be without her now.
Not until I make a dissolution:
I have no daughters.

FOR CHRISTMAS

Hubble shows us this:
the star factory in Sagittarius
where time's a flying strand
looping from a furnace

where, out of the flux, out of the fire,
a boilover of hydrogen and sulphur,
cobalt and vermilion
from the radiant debris,

a scatter of new stars
streams out, seeds of light.
Pinpricks in our darkness:
guides as good as any for the journey.

INBETWEEN

Violet Catherine Lloyd, 1896-1947

Jangle and smash of breaking glass
make a wound I fall through
to the steps inbetween
kitchen and wash-house
where milk bottles went flying
when the clot in her brain
tripped the hurrying blood
and she crashed

on the three steps inbetween
where I kicked at the milk crate
nine summer weeks later
and lay down to play dead
snuffling sour milk and mildew,
the cold of the slate
closer than arms.

Her feet stuck up like islands
or tree stumps under snow.
Her food was white stuff,
not-milk, its smell of rusty nails
dug up in flowerbeds. Once
I had to hold the feeding cup
she sucked at blurrily, like a sick kitten.

She didn't speak our language any more.

Some of what she'd left forty years behind
in the hills above Cilfaesty
caught up: jerked out words
that slowly started to make sense,
became what I at four could salvage
and now give breath to daily:
gwely, fy ngharaid, cysgu.

Bed, my darling, sleep.

REBUILDING

They called him Mister Vee and said he had
green fingers. That was why I watched him first.
I can still hear the tap and scrape of tines
working all day making a garden
from the wastelands outside our windows.
Soon as I woke, I looked to find him there.

When he saw me between the curtains, he would give
a little stiff-backed bow or lift the rake
with his good hand. He greeted me from school
with a nod of pleasure or congratulation.
He'd gesture at worked ground or present
newsprint flowers, folded small.

We never spoke and so I never knew he had
no English. Sometime late in autumn
they buried him. I was not supposed to understand
though I looked out every day
on deadness. Only as I watched the sun
rousing bulbs he'd planted gravely in straight rows

I began to learn who – what – he had been
before they found him hanging in the shed
where tidily he'd put himself away
each evening after bread and cheese
at somebody's back door. Just a D.P.
my mother said, nowhere to go and nothing left.

I saw them, after, the Displaced Persons,
drifting past, listless, too tall
for the thin brown jackets or shoddy skirts
they had been issued. Grey faces, empty
or too-eager. Always wanting work. Their eyes
turned dark as they locked on to playing children.

They disappeared in winter, like the birds,
like the stray cats in the bomb-site weeds.
We got a fence, tea-roses, a spaniel puppy.
At school we practised for the Festival of Britain.
With oilcloth squares of red and white and blue
my Brownie pack spelt out 'Prosperity'.

WATCHING SKYLARKS

Though they soar and loop and hover
hundreds of feet, dot
and dizzy-canyon-high,
chipping, off blue air,
song that cascades to earth
glittering like meltwater

strings finer than belief
keep them pegged back to the ground
a plummeting downspiral
to the breast-turned hollow
where three still-silent eggs
stare at the sky.

BLUEBELLS IN NANHORON

Y gwyllt atgofus persawr
Yr hen lesmeiriol baent
– R. Williams Parry, *Clychau'r Gog*

Their rising unlatches the season.
Bright as flesh, as easy bruised, they gather
even in snow, shards of a mirror

where other selves drunk on their honeys
harvest and grieve over armfuls
or, dubbed with sap in their deep cool bed

dizzy-ringed with love and deep-vein blue
hug a slow way home as the hardfaced moon
melts and lies down in the whispering aisles.

Like ours, their roots are naked. Bare as tubes
not gripping or resisting, they suck
last year's sugar, feed this summer back.

Slowly the canopy closes.
In its caves, birdsong first echoes
then falls hushed. Curt with seed

The dry stalks rattle, ended. Yet this afternoon
a letter tells me *Driving Mother back*
to the Home in Wolverhampton

by Nant we stopped and wound the windows down
so she might smell the bluebells.
We could not tell if it was now she'd seen

or a wood long bulldozed under, but slow tears
rinsed her eyes and she cried out
of blue, like mist, and special sharp-edged green.

For an hour she talked with sense and without pain
of lives and places eighty years behind.
We never thought so much could have remained.

SILVER WEDDING

for Selwyn and Mim, and i.m. Haydn

Fifteen of those years they've slept
under sharper stars by the Southern Ocean
and woken to the kookaburra's shriek.
There have been other sons; now grandchildren
call them from white sands to winter.

In a different Britain, on their last night 'home'
clenched in a hush of ice
dark-silvered like a mirror
dry wakeful long into the small hours
the couple see at their uncurtained window

a blurring rush of white

(thud, scrabble as of reaching)

the hooded glimmer of a white owl's eyes

and from memory's adjoining room
with its door that never will stay closed

they hear the dead child singing.

THESAURIAN

Cache.
Stook, rick, stack;
Cage, pen, hutch, stall, sty.
Kist, larder, pantry, store,
Buttery, still-room, cellar, ice-house.
Lanary, granary, warehouse, barn.
Safe, repository, strong-room, vault.
Coffer, reserve, portfolio.
Library, gallery, museum, menagerie.
Litter-bin, lumber-room, slagheap, dump.
Clinic, infirmary, hospital, asylum.
Armoury, arsenal, stockpile. Silo.

Bunker.

POSTCARD

If this were a film....
Long shot of approaching train.
Martial music. Cut to faces.

Poplars screen the furnaces
but the view is mostly what our parents might have seen:
blank horizons, scrub struggling into leaf.
Pools of scum reflect a coffin-lid sky.
Wind from the steppes moans round the crumbling brick.

If this were a novel
it would be cathartic recollection
in a hotel bedroom or smoky fifties cafe
pages of blocked monologue
somewhere towards the middle.

A youth stands guard over a small fire of litter.
Curling headlines, chocolate wrappers, a child's red glove.
Flames here burn thin and cold.

If this were a nightmare
we could hope to understand ourselves through it.
We flock here to look and shudder and walk away
stunned by embers.

But the rows of bunks are rough as cattle stalls,
limewash homely as the barns of childhood.
(Even in the interests of authenticity
you could not expect them to expect us to endure
the smells of fear.) Wire at the windows. Clenching cold.

Cleaners' brooms and buckets rattle.
There's an irritation in the eyes like ash.
Sulphur from the smelters in Katowice:
dusk thickens early in this poisoned air.

If this were the history of a civilisation
it might be a footnote, towards the end.

IN THEIR CHAINS

Three days from the railhead, in another forest
a whisper shivered through us like a breeze:
It's Christmas Eve and suddenly
men's voices, singing,
swept towards us and embraced us.

I was singing, Gretchenyn was singing,
anyone who had the breath for it
was singing. The tune was
Holy Night, in whatever childhood words
it had been learned.

Then someone started on the Polish lullaby.
I choked on it. Bile burned my throat.
The voices faltered, faded, died.
The bare trees went on staring.
Soon afterwards we walked into
our second blizzard. I was one
who somehow stumbled through.

THE SCENT OF GERANIUMS

for Helen Bamber

Her office where the Commandant had lived
looked out on silver birches, a field of wildflowers.

By then the huts had all been burnt.
She walked in the woods at twilight, after work.

Birdcalls all of finding, green buds butting light,
but over everything the smell of burning

and something darker, sweeter, like geraniums
crushed in the hand, that she cannot forget.

Her job, at twenty, to heal bodies.
What she learned was how to venture

how to lead a journey back
into the wasteland where the words

can scarcely breathe, to bear witness
so victims can be ordinary, reprieved.

She grows geraniums in pots now
on the balcony of her London flat.

Sometimes, slips out of the warm lit room
to touch the flowers and smell her fingers

not knowing whether it is a wish to forget
or a need to remember

that persistent breath of earth, dark honey
and decay: the bright flower

and its black, our symbiotic truth.

4TH JUNE, BEIJING

Today, remembering it might be
imprudent to wear white or carry a flower
or recite a poem called April

breathes on the embers
of those six weeks like a spell
of pure light leading to summer

and trembles spirit wings
(as in the night of their cages
trapped larks and orioles

wait for unhooding,
trusting the buried grains of desire
to sprout with new green).

Today, old men from the alleys
lift their faces to the sun.
They swirl cages through the air

and smile as the brush of wind
pierces the park with shrill cries:
rehearsals of freedom.

AT LOS ALAMOS

1945

I. Arlene

From her room in the sanatorium
daily letters full of jokes and dreams:
the little boy they had made only
in their heads, who might still be waiting
with his sisters, to be fetched
she wrote, like apples in a loft

reached Box 1663 behind the double fence
round the blankfaced buildings on the mesa
where he watched the last snow glisten
on the Sangre de Cristo mountains,
formulae churning like colours in his mind.

Twice a week he drove across the desert
to sit beside his wife, not teasing her now
of Einstein's dictum that matter was a blemish
in the electron dance. She quoted Marvell:
he spoke of harnessing the sun.

And drove back to his calculations.

A red dress she would have liked to wear
caught his eye from a shop window
four months later and for the first time
he wept, remembering how
after the last small breath, he'd stared
an hour at her travel clock, stopped.

II. Finding Out

Two weeks after the funeral
the message came: *Baby expected*
Jornada del Muerto
16th July, at dawn.

Lightning turned the desert to a set.
The air was thick, like breathing
graphite. He sweated as they waited
in the dark. Three busloads of troops
drove past and an army weapons carrier
pulled over while one soldier
stumbled into bushes, retching.

Feynman fiddled with the radio
searching the ether for instructions.
Only static, then a burst
of music, waltzing, *Sleeping Beauty*
tinny-sweet and shocking. He swore
and worked the dials again.
Still nothing. As he shrugged, starting
to walk away, a male voice rasped:
Minus 30 seconds. All lie face down...
and then the hiss of isolation.

So he could claim he never heard
the order not to look.
His were the only human eyes
to witness that first bleaching flash
that took the place of dawn
at five twenty-nine and forty seconds.

It turned the earth as white as ash,
sky silver, lemon, then vermilion
as clouds boiled and a fireball stretched
across three miles of sky. And then

the blast: *It pounced, it bored its way*
right into you as air's shell cracked
like solid thunder. Deliverance:
they'd talked of how the seams
of all existence might be torn apart.

In the strange stretched quietness after
his eyes came back in focus
on a spider, its body jewelled
by dawn and dewfall, clambering
over and through its sandgrain world.

What a wild night we had, after.
I remember playing bongo drums
on the bonnet of a colonel's jeep.

It was a game for us, the fun
of finding out. We were just kids.

It was a year later, in New York
in a restaurant on Fifty-Ninth St with his mother
when the shockwave swamped him and he saw
how the maths had wrapped him, kept him blind.

SHELLEY SOLVING THE GREAT RIDDLE

Bay of Lerici, August 1822

However far down
you fall slowly towards the sea floor
you hear the storm

in the moving silence
the reds and greens and purples
sway to and fro

you feel the yield and release
of the stem you are clinging to
but no resistance

your body's sealed in silver;
magnetised, sure as a needle
suspended

water takes your weight
lifts hair to life like seaweed
there is no hurry in it

it will only idly turn the pages
of the book you have let fall face down
on old revenges, tendernesses;

its words will be washed away
its black cover beaded with light,
stilled to coral

and now
the small fish
look up as they pass and nibble
at the bright chains

of your visiting breath
floating up towards the light
bubbles that leave you

your life-breath
leaving you behind.
So this is what it's like.

SURVIVOR

Three sisters at bay, and between them
the brother who scrubbed himself out.
Three governesses, pale in dark dresses.
It might be for the prospectus they planned:
their Establishment of Young Ladies.
(Mrs Mangnells' Questions and the pianoforte.)

The eyes especially give nothing away.
Full-mouthed Emily stares out past us.

After supper, pacing the parlour
like creatures not yet compromised
by captivity, their shadows passing
between lamp and window
regularly as a ploughing team, they rolled back
day's horizons and 'made alive'
worlds they blossomed in, Gondal and Angria.

Moments so dark as these
I have never known –
Charlotte, after searching the frozen moor
for an enduring sprig of heather
so Emily could hold one as she died.

Emily who had fed them all
and wrestled Branwell into bed,
starved the prison of her body
for a coffin sixteen inches wide
in the darkest days of winter.

Keeper whimpered in the pew.

Five months later, Anne
on the alien dry coast she chose:
I should regret to have lived
for so little purpose...

Charlotte felt the one locked out.
Life is black, brief and bitter.
But found she could make live again:
steered Shirley with her mastiff Tartar
safe at last to a wedding haven.

Love, like a glass too many
of after-dinner wine, blurred her.
With her dull 'dear boy' curate
she had too her sixth-month flowering.
Then retched herself and half-formed child
into the barren dark beneath the yews
where rooks called mockery
to the father, nine-times-bereft
Bronte, survivor.

PLATH

When the mirror on the wall
looked at her, and winked,
she wanted to be the inverse,
the smug twin looking out;

to cut off her head and hang it
in a gilded frame, to be
the wicked queen for all to see;
to fall in love all over again

with the world, like a baby,
like the goose that drinks the moon.
To be the looking glass,
not through it.

PHANTOMS OVER WALES

Wales as the Phantom fighter pilot flies
could be crouching, wounded
backed up and bayed, but still fighting.

Another way, it's collared
and survives by dancing.

Llŷn is its foreclaw, clenched, or perhaps
one of Branwen's empty arms
on the made-barren belly of the Irish Sea.

But mainly a codenamed constellation:
swooped valleys and mountains, towns
glittering on his screen.

A pattern of targets.

ADJUSTING THE FOCUS

Where I was then seemed always out
in the cold, or locked in with it.
Never since such an Antarctic
numbness, ice-caves, walls
of whiteout where giant voices
boomed unfocussed warnings.
My own throat was tight with frost,
time a glacier in an iron gorge.

So I tried to twist my self
still smaller, quieter, a dot
kept close within a code
of scratch marks, twiggy syllables.
Through words I found a wormhole
I came through to womanhood
that floodplain with its fruiting trees,
the dance of air and water
their voices, low, loosening.

Between two arms of the sea
I have stood, companioned,
pliant, in a greenfern nest.
But now something stronger in me rises
sweating out the fester
baking fear to a dry ache.

It will leave me light as pumice
that survives
sandblasts, tides of heat;
a recognition in the desert
throwing light back from the edge
of an old drained sea

till, unclenched, windlifted
over hill forts and concrete pinnacles
wafted to a view of forest,
I dream the canopy
where pollination hums. And further out:

to where the blue-white swirling
world, its continents cloud-swaddled,
its oceans blossoming, fills
the whole horizon, spinning
every ninety minutes
as the space-walker hangs

in an imminence of plummeting
in an eternity of star-pricked dark

for a moment looking down
to where her children might be
stirring out of sleep, then back
to the job, to unscrew the bolts
on one of Hubble's golden wings,
watch it fall away and shimmer into flame

but for a moment seeing clear
how one day, opening arms wide, she will
(I will)

joyously or with regret
let this self go.

*The final reference is to astronaut Dr. Kathryn Thornton who
took part in the NASA mission to repair the Hubble space telescope.
She worked for two hours 'hanging like a bat' from the end of a long
remote-controlled arm to release a damaged solar array.

ON THE TRAIN FROM CHESTER

So, now I'm teaching people how to die,
announces the tweed-hatted woman
to her friend fighting the *Telegraph*
for the crossword page. Closing her eyes

she intones: *Let the red spark*
dance over an open fire
and dissolve like smoke
into the calm of clear light.

Lie down, I say, on your right side
in the sleeping lion posture.
Rest and gaze at the sky like a window.
Let your mind go, let your clenched self go.

Breathe in peace, breathe out love.
Loosen all sensation in your fingertips
and toes, slow down the pumping heart.
Feel how the edges disappear.

The dark syllable of your thought,
the red spark of your passions;
let them fade, flow out,
just drift away...

I buzz, must butt in. *But does it work?*
They fell me with a look
and stiffen to their magazines. Furiously
I scribble on the flyleaf of my Pepys

in case the instructions come in useful.

TALKING IN THE DARK

Now the air is indigo with evening
together by the boathouse where we've sprawled
an hour or more, felt earth's breath cooling,
we wake mind-echoes of 'the real world'.
Night prompts us all to visions of tomorrow.

A subtle fullness, like a ripening field
contains us, names and knowledge weightless now.
The biosphere, Helen thinks, might still have the power
to heal pillage, maiming, poison. Protests fly:
excuse for doing nothing, weak, evasion.

Although we can't agree what should be done
a tribal dignity begins to hover.
Shadows with eyes that hold the light, we are
communicators, not just talking faces.
First stars beckon in a deepening sky.

The universe accepts our hopeful voices
but sea demurs with one slow-hushing sigh.

MRS CRUSOE

Each time she wakes
she is clinging to
him, as if the storm they surge through
is a visitation, not
of their own making, and they are no more than
victims of the gale that wrecks
the world and howls at their black window.

But his arms will not
close round her, and each time
she reaches over it is like
touching stone or someone
she has killed. Warmth grows
under her hand but it is not response:
cells' chemistry, no answer.

Her eyes are full of grit,
her face stiff with the salt
she has not bothered
to wipe off. She turns away
into the seaweed of her hair
and lets sleep take her
down below the slap of feeling.

Perhaps the words will not set hard.
Morning may be another bright new shore
where they wake above the tideline, strangers
with clear eyes, eager and exploring smiles.

HARVEST

Oat stooks in rows across the field
Between the Vikings' ridge and furrow
And ruins of the abbey tower
Are patient straggle-headed pilgrims
In short, coarse tunics. Three weeks
Of sun and wind they have to wait
Tidy groups of five or seven
That lean closer in the moonlight
Whispering under that wide island sky
Where all the clouds seem harvested.

Some days we walk out among
The quiet procession, turning each
To face the sun. Grasped firmly by the waist
They crackle, crisp with starch. When
They're dry to shining, like new wings,
They are ready for the next part of the ritual.

The mountain celebrates in its purple
On the day we harvest, and the east wind's woken
So the sheaves we gather and toss up
Are snatched, and lift a little from the fork
So that for a second, angel after stubby angel
Takes flight and flies, stiff-skirted, to the trailer.

In the threshing barn with both doors open
Blown husks swirl, spiralling
As once they rose through sodden earth,
Then, waste, they lie down
For the mice and the scavenging birds.
Their whole life was movement:
They were a rustling congregation,
Each stalk a tiny steeple with a dozen bells.
How willingly the crop bent to the binder
Like water pulled straight to the brink
Not dead, like cropped hair, but flowing,

A weft stretched to its unweaving,
Its winter-long unravelling

The sheaf from the stook, from the stack
In the barn, the grain in the husk
In the belly in the byre
In the maw of a bird over Africa
Strings tossed, new-tying,
In the breath of the world.

Tonight, the sea leans hard
On the island, bringing cold rain
And firstfall of winter thrushes to the stubble.
But all evening our minds are lifted
By the high ride home, the field clean
Of shadows, and the full barn.
We feel our faces burn, our skin
Is restless, eyes dry-rimmed, as though
Our bodies too are practising, itching
To learn the lovely grace of letting go.

BEFORE THE BELL

A child, I knew flesh was a chrysalis.
One day would come the sense of stretching
wings, the warmth of setting colours
drying to a glass. It is May –
the extrovert month. Another hatching's done.
I launch myself along the morning corridors

and meet a choreography
of signalled urges. Enclosed as underwater
shoals, grown children flick and dart and hover
in patterns mysterious as magnets,
gametes' swirl of shrieks and chatter.
Enriched by longing and the summer light

eyes variously bright as sea-anemones
beckon, as deceitful-smooth.
Skin's flushed, translucent, clear as fruit
or opening blooms. There's an orchid sulky
in its ripening, a boy whose fine beard hair
turns in the sun to golden floss.

This time before the teachers come
is charged with purpose blind but beautiful.
I clatter past in a bubble of irrelevance
busy, invisible. Turning past the toilets
down the glass passage to the Science block
three girls glide towards me, arms lifted wide

as wings, heads haloed in light
like Veronese saints. Catrin's long red hair
springs out a flame aura, a pirate queen's.
Pierced by prodigal shine, life's energy,
after fifty years I find myself
loving the husk, the dying cells.

GIVING UP

She has a face like a flower,
the mouth already ripening as fruit.

Can I talk to you a minute? That was my last lesson.
Through three terms I have watched her

blossoming, shaping herself
into a summer woman, hunting fun.

Tonight is Parents' Evening but I won't
be seeing hers. She's left home

oh, months ago, moved in with someone
who's moved on now. She shrugs *no problem.*

And, anyway, she's giving up the course. Today.
It's not me, college, all this stuff to study.

She reminds me how – *like one of those
Liz Lochhead poems!* – her mother died

early in the story, and her stepdad's always said
it was up to her to get on any way she could.

She sketches a pattern of used sweetness
I see as degradation, she as growing up

(but on the cusp of recognising
how what we find we can put up with

turns into appetite or what we need).
Then: *I can't help it. I'm just no good.*

*I don't feel I belong to anyone
but I have to be what everybody wants.*

She tells of walking through a mist
of greening trees, wanting to be lost.

Of staring in the mirror till it blurs,
black discs swallowing her eyes – *no me anymore* –

of cutting an arm to red ribbons, of starving
until she doesn't bleed. *I can't cry either.*

All I can give her is a helpline number
and a fiver for something to eat.

My way home is through woods. Driving
with the window down I find I have to watch

cloud floss relentless as feathers
blurring the face of the helpless moon,

hear a seeking cry as it shivers,
dissolving back into the dark again.

NOT MUCH LIKE R.S. THOMAS

I am telling cousin Rozzy on the phone
how I like cleaning the conveniences
in a village with a view of soft green gorsey hills:

how the reassuring smell of Dettol
whisks me back to childhood
and how I savour the frisson

of bustling boldly in with spray and bucket
towards the Gents – "Cleaner coming through!"
That gets them shifted. But claim

kinship with the rubbish men
who rumble up, dash in
with a "Scuse us, love, bit of a rush."

How exotic are the men's urinals,
wide flower mouths I polish
to a giant lily brightness

and turn each lavatory pan
green as a rockpool
livid with algae.

Sounds like a poem coming on
my cousin teases, and sets me thinking:
there are worse jobs for a writer.

You can be silent with your thoughts
or slosh around and sing. Even stop
to scribble if you feel the urge.

Wiping taps and mirrors shiny
you look beyond yourself to catch
characters without their captions,

plot a context for their angry, anguished
messages. Wonder which of them it is
who pinch the soap and moss-green Andrex

why they block the pan with sodden wodges
and whether infant schools do quite enough
free finger-painting and squidging of clay.

"Illuminate the underside," Blake said
the poet should, "be like the glow-worm."
(Must come by late to look for some.)

Mornings though, my company is birds:
songthrush and blackbird, a chiffchaff.
Woodpecker yaffles down by the river.

Young mums plump-bummed in pastel shorts
stop off to let kids wild from playschool
squabble on the swings, squeal in the daisies.

At evening whole families assemble
to watch old men at their bowls
or swap gossip they picked up in chapel.

I think but do not tell about today:
a woman overcome on her way home
with bad news from the hospital

about her husband. In sun-dapple
beneath young sycamores
absently dead-hunting daffodils,

as a stranger I could share her pain
and felt the quickening of a phrase to tune,
a thread that tugs. But Roz is laughing:

Not much like R.S. Thomas, though.

ROUNDING

Here, by this water's rush and
tumble, constant unloading
of itself and spilling to the sea,
you remember. A forefinger creeps
childlike to your lip, as you wonder
when the waterwheel was lost
that churned the elements together
when you leant out to wash your catch
or cup a drink from the rounding pool

(thinking no more than birds
or the bright water what language
you should think in, time easy as air
about you). Next, you make us crouch
to crawl into your small-girl hiding place,
foxhole between giant boulders
a glacier dumped, and we smile at your *Yoohoo!*
waving down the well at our three tiny heads
silhouetted against summer. From far down
darkness breathes rot at us, and you exclaim
at barricades of sloe and bramble
where eighty years ago was orchard.

Anxious that ruin was all you would find
we jibbed at bringing you before. Now
let not hospital nor graveside be
where you are remembered, but each June
nudge us with the fun you had
here, where water that needs never to grow old
hides in the undergrowth, chuckling,
then rounds to look back at the sky
before its long slow falling to the sea.

SAFEWAYS

The yawn of early afternoon's the time you'll see
women just too young or too far to play grannies
slow trolleys that they steer deliberate as prams
between the aisles of snacks in family packs
and ice cream garish in a score of tastes; saunter
alleyways of Pampers and sterilising stuff – even
hang back smiling from the check-out scrum

to study mothers tethered by their infants,
and feel again the tug, that never-sleeping
sense of extension. They know all about
the weariness, the play and sting
of mutual friction: their eyes may be soft
but wryness twists their lips. As long grass
shoots in spring and thickens round

a holed bucket or last year's useful tool
left rusting by the farmyard wall, their kids
have grown through them, moved on.
Good, once, to keep the blades at bay
and make a lee, part of them's still programmed
(keep that bunny jelly mould, those bricks)
for function. Relic status. Rediscovery.

CROSSING FROM THE ISLAND

The wake is a clench
of white muscle

the sea's grey flesh
winces and rears

before the blade
of our bow.

All the way over, you have to
stay upright, keep choosing

to gulp air, to blink salt
and dark away.

The rocks ahead howl.
Horizons tremble, knowing

bubbled alleys wait.
Bladderwrack lifts warty fingers.

And when at last
you step ashore and stand

triumphant and exhausted
drenched, blind

on a new safe shore
look back and see

how the water still
plunges and shudders

wide-staring, mad-frothed
at the mouth

waiting for the next time.

GHOST-DANCE OF THE ISLAND GOOSE

In the year's longest night, roused by the moon
she stretches, widening icebright wings as if to fly
to a dream of wilderness, and clangs out a rallying cry
to the gossiping clan that once clustered round her –
all those husbands and hatchlings who year by year
left her behind, were taken and lost
in snow-flurries of feathers or bone-cracking frost.
Still as death lie the fields. But she's not alone
with her ghosts and her bag-woman mutterings:
all around her the sea, its beat steady, like wings.

CONTROLLING

Hunter strides back beaming from the nets.
At his belt, a dozen small cloth bags
hang like fruit, but throbbing.

His hand curls round warmth,
a tremble of feathers, a bright head
firm between first and middle finger.

*A male, quite old. See how the wingtips
are worn?* He spreads the brown wing wide
like an X-ray scanning the web of lift.

He breathes on the down of the breastbone
to measure yellow fat. Checks data –
calculates its chances of survival.

I see a leg thinner than the thinnest wire,
a round eye in a clench of strangeness
and realise why tales of alien abduction

are all too much the stuff of ordinary fears:
conscience pangs of a controlling species.
Caught and held, investigated by a being

so beyond imagination, the brain
would seize, the memory cells
crash, milky with unrecognition.

It takes time when the hand opens
for the goldcrest to untrance, to feel
bright air unfolding, and to fly.

*To the ornithologist, re-trapping and recording a bird
already ringed is 'controlling'.

GOING OVER

It's full summer. Neither of them
sleep well. They blame the heat,
work problems, the late and early festival
of thrush and blackbird in the garden
they have made together.

They don't eat much either. Walls
lean in towards them. He reads
the front page of last week's *Chronicle*
over and over while she sits to stare
at ants foraging across the sill
till her coffee has gone cold or to watch
ivy ripped from the apple tree
struggle to die. Its sharpnesses
glitter until after sunset.

He thumps and clatters
in the shed. She bakes and boils
and fries. These are the busynesses
they hide inside. He'll clean the car, repair
a fence. We must cut these hedges back
she says, let in air, make room for growth.

In bed they edge out of each
other's warmth or move
too deliberately near so skin
rasps nervelessly where it should
slide and smooth. Letting breath out's
difficult. He coughs. Her throat
tightens. In the sweaty dark

she struggles to clear gulps
clogged in a clenched black tube
that seems to want to starve
and stiffen. She is fighting it,
not him. A sickroom gentleness
trembles between them
as they wait for light to break

as another morning breaks.

LIGHTNING

There's a new colour you can almost see,
taste of hot tin, a furnace door ajar.
The cat is tense, black fur
electrified. Willow rods
leap in the hands like dolphins.

When lightning threatens
turn clocks and mirrors to the wall

hide all your knives,
loose glass and shiny surfaces

switch off the radio and tv
and all appliances greedy for the thrill.

It would be too much for them.

Douse the fire, put butter and cream
in the dark: underground is best.

Leave back doors slightly ajar
and never shelter under trees.

Get out of the water. Get off
the boat, but stay in your car.

Crouch, unless your skin is tingling
and hair's on end, then drop. Lie prone.

Cover your head
and watch out for your eldest daughter.

Count the seconds.
Wait for the thunderbolt.

There are people with burn marks
on the top of their head
and the soles of their feet:
those the lightning has passed through.

Struck individuals
have a special sensitivity,
my acupuncturist says
as he taps the shining silver needles in
at wrist and ankle, crown of the head.
Too much of a price to pay.

OUT OF SEASON

for Maura Maguire, painter.

I

She brought to mind Eurydice
wintering through the dark alone

lying along the cold spine of an island
where she planted herself among the used-up things –

bleached grass, bracken-rust, ghosts
of twenty thousand pilgrims in the fog

rhizomes under the earth
already tightened to cold fists

all those mouths that might burst open in mute earth,
those cold bones waiting to be changed –

as if she'd filled pockets with stones
and sunk

into the burying, moonless dark
where in winter not even birds or seals will sing:

there's only the sea's white-lipped aching
under a wind-scratched sky.

II

When the radio batteries gave out
she sat and listened to the wind

banging round outside, like a caller
nervous of the dark, reminding her

of all the empty spaces in the world.

Lying on her pallet under the bare slates
she spoke her own name into the moonless dark,

once stumbling down the stairs to light a candle
to breathe at the face in her own hand mirror

putting a finger to it to make sure
she was more than a dream of a painting herself.

And in the lull heard redwings whistling overhead unseen,
the wingbeats of two hundred birds

wheeling as a single force
keeping contact and the vision steady

of safety, rest, sweet water, through the dark.

III

At Candlemas she starts to paint again –
moments of passing lit with luminous desire,

a glow of becoming: cupped hands turn to
a chalice, a darkfaced angel

lifts a heart like a newborn, like a fruit
holding all the seeds of history,

roses grow wild round a deserted tower
and a blind boy confidently carries his song

across a shattered landscape, under an anxious sun.
In all, the sea glitters as if just unbound.

And now at last she writes her letters home,
laughs as she asks me to stamp them for New York.

BEFORE FULL REASON WAKES

Badger screams in the sunken hours
tear the thinning layers of my sleep
so for four stunned
thuddings of the heart

there is only fear under a frosty sky,
the throb of blood
in vulnerable flesh. One last whinny
savages the night like lightning

and mutters away, over the field,
through the stream (I follow
in imagination) and along
gorse tunnels to the mountain.

I hardly believe in the self I come back to
the luxurious warmth I lie rolled in,
this too-large empty den
and this presumptuous, feeble body.

From the Maths Room wall I remember
Curves of Pursuit, the plotted course
of one animal chasing another.
Right paw first draws a spiral clockwise;

widdershins pricks angles like alert ears.
Unclenching into drowse, my mind
patters through, and over and over
those knots of purpose, geometric flowers,

the predictable and ancient patterns
adrenalin and woken instinct trace.

THE MARINER'S LAST MESSAGE

His voice jerks out from the recorder
found carefully plastic-wrapped,
on the yacht ghosting towards home:

I've met monsters you wouldn't believe.
Small ones, but –
Clare must not –Repeat NOT
come to the Scillies to meet me.

Tell her –I wanted her to be proud of me.
I wanted to win, so I agreed.
I've been given these words to say.
I can't say them to her.

May she be spared the pain, may
our children grow to comfort
and console, to give her
what he will not even let me name.

But what a shameful secret, what a trick
he used! If only we had seen
that this perfect shining instrument – this boat –
was a message – a riddle to be worked out.

The name alone says it all:
Electron – it's the mystery
we've tampered with. None of us
suspected. Now I have to pay.

I have to play. It's a little game.
He has given me the mind
of a second generation cosmic being,
and I see it all.

The quick are quick and the dead
are dead. No, no, I could not endure

*more waiting, the terrible water,
the creatures in it, writhing.*

*The water is black. It is waiting.
I am safe inside the pentagram
drawn in rope across the deck.
It's the bargain. Once I step beyond*

*it is finished. It is as good as finished.
It is the mercy. It's the eleventh hour.
Eleven hundred hours, fifteen minutes, no seconds.*

It is the end of my terrible gamble.

Eleven hundred hours, seventeen minutes.

Is it time already?

*No seconds for me
when I make my move.*

*I'll do it, damn you!
Eleven hundred hours, twenty minutes,
forty seconds.*

*I know, there can only be one
perfect beauty; only one chess master.
But I will play this game as I choose.*

*For God's sake, remember the riddle.
Save yourselves. Remember the game.*

And then only the hiss
of the machine, water's empty slap.

*The yacht Teignmouth Electron was discovered abandoned in July 1989 after
losing contact for several weeks in the Round the World yacht race. Its skipper
Donald Crowhurst was never found.

ESTUARY

From safe ground, watch
the turning of the tide at flood:
mullet rise to nibble light while
almost drowned, samphire shifts
and sweats. Five widgeon
whump themselves into the air,
weighed down by water
and their own reflections, dragging.

Beached so high it's moored
by brambles, the skeleton
of a small boat rocks in sand.
Its clinker split, its joints unpicked,
the blue wishbone of its keel
points seaward still.

Sky's prayer flags bleach
and fray. As if it is
the last one in the world
a curlew sings kaddish. Salt
goes on eating the rusting iron ring
where infinitely slowly
lichen creeps across the seawall.
Think migrations of the sediments;
the way continents slide.

Now land breathes again. It is the ebb.
But go on watching. This time
will be different. Or you will.

SWIMMERS

April 6, 1998

In celebration of Elwyn Evans and George Povey,
lobstermen and boatmen to Bardsey island who died,
aged 39 and 49, within a month of each other.

Irish Sea, Shannon: North-easterly 4-5; fair, good.

One's flooded, awash,
Struggling but focussed, all verb,
Every cell alive and tingling;

One's plugged in, enclosed,
Safe in a hull of light
But drifting away.

One dark, one fair. Of an age,
Boatmen of the same bay in the same sea.
It is their workplace. Their battleground.

Journeying souls, how many times have they
Shivering, rowed out from the dark
Into the wide arms of a sunlit sea?

How many mornings, pulling pots,
Stood balanced against dawn and seen
Their own shadows floating in the lee?

Like the old sailors, they steered
By instinct, reading the sea's pulse
Through the soles of their feet.

Slack water.

Beached on a white bed, castaway
Of tidal surge or slow erosion,
Some linkage in his brain torn loose,

The golden man lies still as coral,
Ghost-fished by his own neurones.
All night, all days, his wife keeps vigil.

To her half-closed eyes, his body
Patterned with sunlight through the curtains
Ripples, lifts as if awash

As if the sea has crept right up
To embrace him even here and wash his face
With brightness, dress him with white foam.

He dreams his workshop with the smells
Of resin, timber, paint. Skips years to scrambling
In an apple tree, scrumping with his gang.

Then he's a hero on a makeshift raft
Alone and racked with thirst and heat.
He is a baby crawling on dark velvet

Tide on the turn, flooding.

Adrenalin tells George *this can't be happening.*
His hands slice through each wave
Feeling its weight, stroking its power

Cupping its glitter in his palms to push it
Back behind him, and some more, and more.
With each inbreath, he leaps

Rides the sea like a dolphin, thrust and glide.
He knows he cannot hurry. Thinks how long
A store-pot takes, simply sinking down.

A strong swimmer, he's always been.
Known for his push, his energy.
But already he cannot feel his legs.

Again he reaches, forward, down, round.
Recalls how swallows swing in loops
Of golden air, swoop low over water

And he is playing his first salmon
In the dark pool of Llyn Golchi Defaid
Where trees are budding into sharp green leaf.

Half-flood: tide-rip, wave-crest, roller.

Elwyn on the white bed dreams
Sunlight busy with a brisk north-easter. Cold,
Off the land. River freshness in his mouth.

His body seems buoyed up by weight of water
Floating face down in a rock-pool, brilliant
With tiny winking bubbles, jewel anemones

No longer on the mooring in the dark
Trapped in uncertainties between
A roughening sea and the huge effort

Of hauling out and driving home.
Vague-faced as a summer cloud he's been
A year and more, as stunned, or listening.

Four hours flood: ground-swell, curler, surf.

Wind puffs at the water, wakens him
In a mirror shattered to a million fragments.
He moves again, and there are two of him

One still sitting on the upturned hull
Thinking *bloody fool*, shouting it, watching him
Struggle, slowing, towards shore, risking it.

He has been so long in water
The two-thirds of him that is salt
And pull of tides, is dreaming him.

He reaches forward, willing fingers' grip,
Legs to bend and thrust, but he is flying now
Not swimming, he has lifted off –

All the days of his life stroked through him
Like moonlight, as he sweeps and rocks,
Slow-over-arms into this element.

High water: ground-swell, surge, seethe, reach.

He is lying on a bed in hospital.
Visions shiver, warp and spindle:
He hears his children's smothered weeping.

He is pressing his head against glass
The cool of a window as the first drench
Of a thunderstorm patters.

By now each time he rolls his head to breathe
Is harder, with a booming roar. Sun
Sticks needles in his eyelids and lungs burn.

He is cradling his newborn daughter.
He is scrambling in an apple tree.
He is a baby crawling through dark velvet.

High water: surge, fetch, swamp.

George head down in the water dreams
Each of his children, his wife's sweet face,
Her fingers dipped in holy water

Stroking across his forehead and down
Held to his lips that shape a prayer
Protect them, and *safe passage*

And sees a sudden candle under water
Glowing brightness in the friendly dark
A home he's known but has forgotten.

Ebbing: foam, sheen, settle.

Elwyn will follow next dark moon
Drifting out in a warm drowse
Curled round his future's still unfolded bud.

There are gull cries on a lift of wind.
Spindrift's blown petals, storm petrels
Like dark butterflies that flit and skim

Against horizon's silver,
Stillness at the furthest edge of light
Ahead of all partings, beyond all farewell.

Swash.

Hic finis chartae viaeque
The old maps used to say.
This is where the known ways end.

* 'swash' – the thin glisten of water that coats the sand
when the tide has gone out.

EXODUS

Leaving the island, 1925

Salt on the lips, honey in the nostrils
from pasture plumped with thrift in bloom.

Last oystercatchers' whistles drown
as sure oars splash, the lugsail creaks.

Only shadows on the mountain now.
They point to where the boats are heading

away from the sun, whose low red light
winks from empty windows, safe-held quartz.

Passing close under Craig yr Adar
its sheer rock fall, its close-packed nests

Tomos calls back all the times he has been
dizzied down on a spray soaked rope.

He cups his hand to a remembered shape,
the gathered egg: blood warmth, silk and grit.

Brittle, but shaped to survive passage.

THE WHIRLPOOL ARM

Braich-y-Pwll

It will see us out,
this reach of rock where water
slows, then simmers.

Here, the centre of the earth
belched granite

that flowed in a bright river
flaring with fire.

Cooling, hunched itself to knuckles
a spine against the ice
carrying the pulse resist
down six hundred million years

so we can stand and watch the Irish sea
swing itself slowly
in
and out

like an undecided summer glacier,
like the slow migrations of the flesh

and on the far horizon's rim
where each day disappears in dark –

ghost fire, dancing.

Acknowledgements

Acknowledgements are due to the editors of the following publications where some of these poems first appeared: *Poetry Wales, Planet, New Welsh Review*.

'Giving Up' was commissioned for *Blodeuwedd*, edited by Edward Cusick (Headland, 2001); 'Bluebells in Nanhoron' appeared in *Making Worlds*, edited by Schneider, Wood & Coles (Headland, 2003). 'Post-card' appeared in *War: An Anthology*, edited by Dewi Roberts (Gwasg Carreg Gwalch, 2002). 'Rebuilding' was commissioned for *Are you talking to me?* edited by Mairwen Prys Jones (Pont, 1994).